VICTORIA

AND SOUTHERN VANCOUVER ISLAND

by

Chris Cheadle

VICTORIA AND SOUTHERN VANCOUVER ISLAND

Canadian Cataloguing in Publication Data
Cheadle, Chris, 1957-
A Portrait of Victoria and Southwest Vancouver Island
ISBN 1-55153-130-5 (bound) -- ISBN 1-55153-131-3 (pbk.)
1. Victoria (B.C.)--Pictorial works. 2. Vancouver Island
(B.C.)--Pictorial works. I. Title.
FC3846.37.C53 1997   971.1'28   C97-910019-4
F1089.5.V6C53 1997

10 9 8 7 6 5 4 3 2

Altitude Green Tree Program
Altitude will plant in Canada twice as many trees as were
used in the manufacturing of this product. This unique
program was created and developed exclusively by
Altitude Publishing in 1995.

Production:

Art Direction and Design	Stephen Hutchings
Editorial Assistant	Sabrina Grobler
Editor	Yvonne Van Ruskenveld
Financial Management	Laurie Smith

Printed in Canada by
Friesen Printers Ltd., Altona, Manitoba

front cover:
Parliament Buildings and Inner Harbour
back cover:
Beacon Hill Park and Gray Whale Tail
page 1:
Victoria Overview
page 2-3:
Victoria's Inner Harbour

Altitude Publishing
1500 Railway Avenue
Canmore, Alberta
T1W 1P6

VICTORIA

AND SOUTHERN VANCOUVER ISLAND

Contents

VANCOUVER ISLAND

Top: Swartz Bay ferry terminal serves as a gateway to the area from the BC mainland and the Gulf Islands.

Opposite: Sidney Island features Sidney Spit Marine Park and kilometres of fine sand beaches, safe moorings, camping, beachcombing, fishing and crabbing.

It is fitting that most visitors to southern Vancouver Island arrive by sea. From the indigenous Coast Salish to the early European explorers, from the gold seekers of the 1800s to the annual Swiftsure sailboat racers today, the sea and ships have constantly shaped life on Vancouver Island.

Relaxing on the ferry as it winds through Active Pass and the Gulf Islands, you get a sense of what islanders love about their home. Gulls glide alongside the passenger decks, cruising for handouts from travelers. White-hooded bald eagles soar from the green walls of Douglas fir and cedar forests. Occasionally, a pod of orcas creates a stir among the passengers. The salt air, sea breezes and time to relax—the whole experience epitomizes the island's allure.

Pleasure craft of all descriptions, fishing boats, work boats and kayaks share the ample bays, beaches and channels. Sailing and yachting, scuba diving, whale watching, sea kayaking, sport fishing, beachcombing, seafood harvesting and even ocean swimming inspire the long and passionate love

Top: Double rainbow over Canoe Cove Marina. The Sidney/North Saanich area features over a dozen marinas.

Left: The Beacon wharf in Sidney is the launching point for the Sidney Island ferry.

Top: BC Ferries' Spirit of Vancouver Island completes its passage through the Gulf Islands as it nears Swartz Bay.

affair locals have with the sea. Visitors too—over 3 million to Victoria annually—fall under the island's spell.

The Mediterranean-type climate of southeastern Vancouver Island and the Gulf Islands comes from the sheltering effect of the mountains of Vancouver Island to the west and the Olympic Mountains in Washington State to the south. The rain shadows of these peaks create one of the driest areas in Canada during the summer; Victoria is BC's sunniest city. The warmest winter in Canada and eight frost-free months mean outdoor activities can occur year round. However, this is the west coast, so rain is often possible and, in winter months, probable.

The southeastern island is surrounded by mountains. The Olympics are to the south and the Cascades are to the east, while the Coast Range to the north is a reminder that snow and skiing are never too far away. The many gentler hills that surround Victoria afford easy-to-vigorous hikes, with striking vistas of the regional lowlands, the sea and the distant mountain ranges.

The open hillsides with their flowering meadows among the Garry oak and arbutus or madrone trees display the region's distinctive ecosystem. The contrast with the vast stretches of verdant rainforest coastline that

Top: A downwind spinnaker run on a crisp winter day. Year-round sail racing and cruising make this area a prime destination for marine enthusiasts.

Opposite: Boundary Channel, with Mount Baker looming in the distance, separates the Gulf Islands to the north from the San Juan Islands in the US.

typifies the north Pacific was evident to James Douglas when he wrote on March 15, 1843, "The place appears a perfect Eden in the middle of the dreary wilderness of the Northwest Coast."

The climate and soils produce elaborate gardens. Hundreds of plant species from around the world have successfully adapted to the mild conditions. Flowering cherries and plums from Japan, California redwoods, Chinese opium poppies and the ubiquitous and pesky Scotch broom are well-established landmarks of the "Garden City."

The Butchart Gardens is the famous showpiece, and the annual Saanichton Fair in early September provides a folksy and impressive glimpse into the farms and gardens of rural Victoria.

With the open meadows, mild climate and the British tradition, it is no surprise that golf evolved as a favourite year-round pastime on the south island. Golfers can try a different course every day of the week in unique settings, from the scenic waterfront Victoria Golf Club to the stately Royal Colwood Golf and Country Club to the challenging Olympic View Golf Club.

Victoria's Inner Harbour and Causeway, surrounded by (clockwise) the Visitors Information Centre in the foreground, the Empress Hotel, the Royal British Columbia Museum and the Legislature.

The 3300 lights tracing the outline of the Legislature each evening provide a storybook backdrop to the popular Inner Harbour. The flotilla of racing yachts awaits the annual Swiftsure Classic.

THE EAGLE
(Kwakiutl, Nootka, Salish)

Vancouver Island first occupied for Britain by Captain James Cook in 1778, became a centre for the fur trade. Named after Captain George Vancouver, the Crown Colony of Vancouver Island was established in 1849 to impress British sovereignty on the West Coast. In 1856 representative government was instituted and a Legislative Assembly elected. It was united with the mainland colony of British Columbia in 1866.

VICTORIA

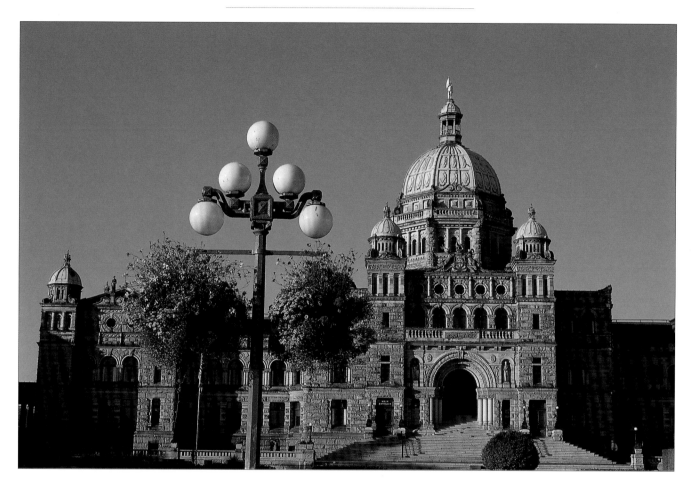

The arrival of the first gold prospectors in April, 1858 roused Victoria from its fur trade routines and transformed it into a lively supply centre. Victoria grew quickly as tens of thousands of people headed for the gold fields of the Fraser River, the Cariboo and the Cassiar.

As Victoria grew and prospered, the genteel customs of aristocratic England took root, such as English country gardens and afternoon tea. Today, the double-decker buses, tea at the Empress, cricket in Beacon Hill Park and the stately Legislative buildings, as well as the understated and polite character of the locals, attest to this British connection.

A summer stroll around Victoria's Inner Harbour is must-do for any visitor. Tourists and locals alike revel in people-watching as street buskers and sidewalk artists delight walkers on the Causeway. Encircled by the Empress Hotel, the Royal British Columbia Museum, the provincial Legislature and Ports Canada wharves, this busy little harbour shelters yachts and kayaks, water taxis and fishing boats, ferries from the US and float planes.

The most visible feature by the Inner Harbour is the domed Parliament Building or Legislature, which opened in 1898. A series of murals at floor level show the early history of European and First Nations contacts.

The Royal British Columbia Museum features realistic natural history exhibits that replicate various provincial ecosystems. Most phases of BC's development, including a mock-up of Captain Vancouver's *Discovery*, scale models of fish canneries and farming, logging and mining exhibits are featured. The First Peoples exhibits which represent the range from prehistory through early contact to the modern age make up the world-renowned anthropological section.

The park allows passersby to admire totem poles of the various First Nations of coastal British Columbia. Mungo Martin House, a copy of a 19th century Kwakiutl chief's house with its distinctive stylized motif, hosts a variety of First Nations functions and dances. The attached carving shed allows visitors to watch Native artists at work.

Across Belleville Street from the museum sits the Empress Hotel. The "Grand Old Dame," bedecked with ivy, features the famous afternoon tea held in its majestic "Tea Lobby."

Top right: Prospectors underscore the profound historical importance of gold exploration and the mining industries.

Top left: Murals by George Southwell adorn the inside of the dome of the Legislature.

Top right: This image of a salmon seiner reflects the lifeblood of coastal British Columbia, the fisheries.

Top left: An ax-wielding lumberjack symbolizes BC's largest industry, forestry.

The Victoria Conference Centre is a modern 1,500-seat facility located behind the Empress on Douglas Street which attracts national and international events.

Bastion Square, site of the original Fort Victoria a pedestrian-only plaza lined with shops and cafes which provides an open-air venue for artisans to hawk their wares.

Market Square was a raucous centre of suppliers, saloons and bordellos for early prospectors. Today the open courtyard of the square, surrounded by 19th century architecture, hosts music festivals and offers interesting shopping and dining.

On Fisgard Street is Victoria's Chinatown, whose secret alleys and false doors contribute to legends of the opium dens and gambling clubs of earlier times. From Pandora Street, you can thread your way through Canada's narrowest thoroughfare, Fan Tan Alley. The elaborate Gate of Harmonious Interest or Tong Ji Men on Fisgard at Government Street and symbolizes the spirit of cooperation between the Chinese and other citizens of Victoria.

Top: Thunderbird Park, with the Empress Hotel beyond, displays totem poles of the First Nations of coastal British Columbia.
Bottom: The Royal British Columbia Museum houses fascinating First Nations exhibits and historical collections, including Captain Vancouver's ship, *Discovery.*
Opposite: Mungo Martin House at Thunderbird Park is a half-scale replica of a 19th century Fort.

Top: Located behind the Empress Hotel, the Victoria Conference Centre hosts national and international events.
Bottom: A horse-drawn carriage ride through old Victoria is a relaxing way to tour the town.

Top: Double-decker buses await tours in front of the "Grand Old Dame"—the Empress Hotel.
Bottom: A highland dancer twirls to the bagpipes. Artists, musicians and buskers delight walkers on the Causeway in the height of the tourist season.

Top left: Swan's Pub at the foot of Pandora Street features colourful flower baskets and boxes.

Top right: The Crystal Gardens is an exotic terrarium housing butterflies, birds and monkeys among its 350 exotic plant species.

Bottom: This decorative entrance on Government Street leads to Bastion Square and the Maritime Museum.

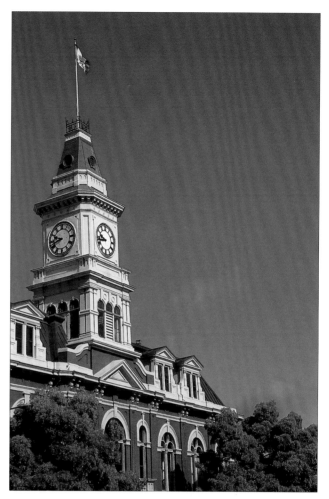

Top left: An eclectic mix of shops and eateries, along with frequent outdoor music festivals, make this quaint and historic site popular.

Top right: Victoria's City Hall was built in 1878; the clock tower was added in 1891.

Bottom: Visitors are treated to a public performance by the Kwakiutl Dancers of Fort Rupert on the Causeway of the Inner Harbour.

Top: Steam-powered vessel at the Classic Boat Festival held every Labour Day.

Top middle: A favourite with children, Undersea Gardens is located in the Inner Harbour and features live Pacific octopus and wolf eels in its displays of indigenous marine life.

Bottom middle: The M.V. Coho departs for Port Angeles, located across the Strait of Juan de Fuca on the Olympic Peninsula.

Bottom: A small boat assures the best seat in the house for the annual Symphony Splash, an early August event that draws over 50,000 supporters.

Opposite: The "Whale Wall" by Wyland at the bottom of Yates Street. Whale watching charters depart regularly from the Inner Harbour in the summer.

Top: Government Street shops offer everything from arts and crafts to tartans and teas.
Bottom: Chinatown along Fisgard Street is another popular shopping and dining area.
Opposite: The Maritime Museum of British Columbia, the former Provincial Court House, sits in Bastion Square.

The newest Gate of Harmonious Interest on Fisgard at Government Street was built in 1981 and recently restored.

VICTORIA AREA

Top: Hatley Castle, now part of Royal Roads University, was considered Canada's finest residence when it was built for James Dunsmuir in 1908.

Opposite: Craigdarroch Castle was built for coal magnate Robert Dunsmuir, but he died before its completion in 1890. You can tour BC's first millionaire's mansion and enjoy the 360-degree view from the turret.

To the west of Victoria's downtown, the Johnson Street lift bridge leads to the newly developed Songhees residential lands. A two-kilometre winding seaside stroll along this tree-lined walkway ends at the West Bay Marina in historic Esquimalt. The Royal Navy began using Esquimalt Harbour in 1848 and today Canadian Forces Base Esquimalt is an important part of the local community.

Across the harbour, another waterfront promenade begins on Belleville Street and affords views to downtown, the Songhees lands and the harbour's entrance. This quiet walkway leads through gardens and behind the Laurel Point Inn to a marina and condominium complex landscaped with exotic gardens and ponds.

Victoria's scenic marine drive begins here in James Bay at Fishermen's Wharf. Past the Coast Guard Station on Dallas Road, the Seattle ferry dock and the shipping terminals, you come to the Ogden Point breakwater. Stretching 750 metres out to sea, it's a favourite spot for walkers, joggers and fishermen. An underwater marine sanctuary along the breakwater

Top: Horse-drawn wagons and carriages carry guided tours through Beacon Hill Park and James Bay.

Bottom: Children love the petting zoo at Beacon Hill Park, which offers ponds and gardens, a putting green, wildflower meadows and the Dallas Road waterfront.

Top: Since 1893, golfers have enjoyed the view from the Victoria Golf Club to the Trial Islands, the Olympic Mountains and the Strait of Juan de Fuca.

makes this the most frequented shore dive on southern Vancouver Island.

East of Ogden Point, the cliffs at Dallas Road send sea breezes aloft, making this a prime locale for kite flying, hang gliding and wind surfing. Beacon Hill Park is just a short walk from downtown. Its wildflower meadows, putting green, petting zoo, playing fields and playgrounds, duck ponds and gardens make it a spacious outdoor setting perfect for a picnic or stroll. At the base of Beacon Hill the coves, beaches and rocky points below the cliffs make for a handy beachcombing location and an ideal spot to explore tide pools.

The scenic oceanside drive continues through Oak Bay and passes through the Victoria Golf Course, whose greens extend right to the water's edge. Farther along is the Oak Bay Marina and Willows Beach, one of Victoria's best swimming beaches. From there, you wind north along the sea to Gyro Park at Cadboro Bay, another well-used beach and playground. Continue driving north to the top of Mount Douglas Park for magnificent views—the city, the Gulf Islands, the mainland lie before you. 🐚

Top: This replica of Anne Hathaway's Cottage, along with its country gardens and other Tudor-style houses, is found at the Olde English Inn in Esquimalt.

Left: Olde English Village and double decker bus.

Top: Craigflower farmhouse on Craigflower Road at Admirals Road was part of a very successful Hudson Bay Company farm and now exhibits 19th century household furnishings.

Bottom: A wall made from beach stones frames a colourful petunia box in Oak Bay.

BUTCHART

Top: With over 50,000 bulbs imported from Holland each year, the springtime tulip displays at The Butchart Gardens are spectacular.

Opposite: The sunken garden is an outstanding feature of the former limestone quarry that is now the famous The Butchart Gardens.

Farther north on the agricultural and suburban Saanich Peninsula, the long, sandy, east-facing Island View Beach is a pleasant walking and picnicking area. At the "top" of the peninsula is Sidney, a vibrant community with a distinctive marine flavour. It boasts both the Washington State and BC Ferries terminals, and with over a dozen marinas in Sidney and North Saanich, thousands of vessels moor in local waters. A new fishing wharf, complete with an artificial reef, will delight fishermen and scuba divers alike. In early December, spectators jam the shoreline to admire the annual Parade of Boats, as the elaborate Christmas light displays on boats large and small glimmer on the sea. Sidney's commercial centre offers shopping, dining and entertainment along Beacon Avenue. For a more complete picture of the community, the Sidney Museum features local history and a fascinating whale exhibit.

Beside a little inlet on the west side of the Saanich Peninsula lies The Butchart Gardens, the most visited attraction in the province. Over 5000 species of flowers and other plants fill a landscape designed over an aban-

Top: These brilliant dahlias are a showy example of the thousands of blooms that emerge each summer.

Right: This monarch butterfly and chrysalis are part of the colourful display at Butterfly Gardens near The Butchart Gardens.

Opposite: The sunken garden mound is surrounded by cherry blossoms, flowers, arbor vitae—with its naturally pruned look—and ivy.

doned rock quarry. Since Mrs. Butchart planted the first flowers in 1904, the grounds have grown to include the showpiece sunken garden and Italian, Japanese and rose gardens. Open lawns with a performing stage, beautiful fountains, statuary, a restaurant and a formal dining room keep visitors engaged for hours while touring the site.

The newly established Gowland Tod Provincial Park runs along the eastern shore of Saanich Inlet almost to Goldstream. This 1200-hectare park with 40 km of hiking trails provides stunning views of Greater Victoria, Saanich Inlet and the Strait of Juan de Fuca. An area of rich biodiversity, it is host to over 100 bird species, as well as cougar, black bear, blacktail deer, mink and otter.

Top: Stellar sea lions and cormorants share a rocky refuge in the Strait of Juan de Fuca near Victoria.
Bottom: A bald eagle extends its talons for a fish meal. Eagles frequent the area and return to the same nest each year.

NATURE

Top: Each summer, transient and resident pods of orcas ply the local waters, here with Mount Baker as a backdrop.
Bottom: Migrating gray whales occasionally stop to feed locally.

MALAHAT

Top: The sweeping vista at the Malahat Summit includes Finlayson Arm and the Olympic Mountains, visible in the distance.
Opposite: Victoria's own Niagara Falls at Goldstream Provincial Park, a delightful hiking and camping facility.

Twenty minutes from downtown Victoria, in Colwood, Fort Rodd Hill Historic Park, Fisgard Lighthouse and Royal Roads University, site of the impressive Hatley Castle, provide a historical perspective in an area marked by meadows, forest and beaches. The neighbouring Esquimalt Lagoon is a prime saltwater habitat for migratory birds. Victoria boasts over 250 bird species as regular visitors, making birding a passion for many.

Witty's Lagoon, farther west along in Metchosin, features a waterfall, an estuary and a lagoon, with long stretches of beach to stroll.

Continuing west along the West Coast Highway provides a wild contrast to the relative calm of the waters closer to Victoria and around the Gulf Islands. A trip to Sooke and beyond offers a sampling of the rugged Pacific beaches and headlands. East Sooke Park, just 40 minutes from Victoria, is an excellent day-hiking area with ocean coves and beaches and kilometres of hiking trails. At Sooke, the Sooke River delights swimmers at the Potholes.

Top: Float home communities, such as this one at Maple Bay, evoke a liberating and nostalgic atmosphere.
Opposite: A glaucus gull hitches a ride with an outgoing crab fisherman.

Top: Mystic Beach, along the newly established Juan de Fuca Trail, makes a delightful day trip from Victoria.

The West Coast Highway winds past smooth-stoned French Beach Provincial Park to the small logging town of River Jordan, a popular surfers' hangout. The town marks the start of the newly established Juan de Fuca Trail, which ends at Port Renfrew. Easy-to-difficult access trails along the highway allow visitors to experience the crashing surf of the Pacific Ocean and pristine beaches such as China or Sombrio, within an hour or two of Victoria. The beaches are best visited when daytime tides are lowest; this is especially true for Botanical Beach at Port Renfrew, with its deep sandstone tide pools. Port Renfrew is the end of the West Coast Highway and the start of the busy West Coast Trail.

CHEMAINUS

Top: The Chemainus Theatre Company's attractive new dinner theatre is one of the 300 new businesses that have opened in the revitalized town.
Opposite: The island's First Nations heritage is celebrated in this Chemainus wall mural, one of over 30 depicting the area's colourful history.

The most scenic way to leave Victoria to the north is to drive along the Gorge Waterway. This long inlet hosts the annual Gorge Rowing Regatta. In spring, the bridge at Tillicum Road and Kinsmen Gorge Park is lined with anglers as the waters teem with spawning herring. From the bridge, a long, tree-lined walkway leads to the Craigflower schoolhouse and farmhouse. This 1856 Hudson Bay Company farm successfully supplied Fort Victoria by ferrying goods the nine kilometres along the Gorge Waterway from Portage Inlet to Victoria Harbour.

Just 19 km north of downtown Victoria is Goldstream Provincial Park, a 150-site provincial campground. The Goldstream River and its saltwater estuary provide a habitat for fish, birds and mammals, particularly interesting during the annual chum salmon run in late fall. Waterfalls, a wide variety of coniferous and deciduous trees, and wildflowers make the park a worthwhile stop at any time.

Beyond the Malahat lies Duncan, where the Cowichan Native Village features the history and artwork of all Vancouver Island First Nations in its

Top left: This finely chiseled totem pole depicts elements of the Kwagiulth cosmology.

Top right: This collection of First Nations artistry is just a small sampling of the rich heritage on Vancouver Island.

Bottom: Visitors to the Cowichan Native Village in Duncan may view works in progress in the carving shed.

Top: Duncan calls itself "The City of Totems" and features a self-guided walking tour to 41 totem poles in the downtown.

exhibits and gift shop. The local Tzinquaw dancers perform beside the Cowichan River at the centre. Yellow footprints painted on Duncan's sidewalks lead you through a walking tour of the town's 41 totem poles by local carvers.

Beyond Cowichan Lake, logging roads lead west across the island to the gigantic rainforest trees at Carmanah Pacific National Park and to the quaint seaside town of Bamfield with its boardwalks and beaches, at the terminus of the West Coast Trail.

Back on the east side of the island, the delightful little village of Cowichan Bay, with its deep harbour, is situated on the Cowichan/Koksilah estuary. Seafood restaurants, hotels and marinas line the waterfront. The Marine Ecology Station invites visitors to view a collection of aquariums featuring mini-habitats of local marine life.

Fifteen minutes north of Duncan lies Chemainus, known as "The Little Town That Did." When slowdowns in the forest industry threatened their town, the residents of Chemainus organized the first Festival of Murals in 1982, which saw the completion of the first five works. Today horse-drawn wagons roll past over 30 historical murals throughout the town, making this Canada's largest outdoor gallery. The completion of the Chemainus

Theatre Company in 1992, featuring first-rate dinner theatre in the 270-seat facility, added the performing arts to the town's growing list of attractions.

Farther north on the Island Highway, Ladysmith sits on the 49th parallel. Transfer Beach Park, below the highway, with its excellent children's playground and picnic area, makes a fine choice for a rest stop. The town's long harbour was created by Robert Dunsmuir as a shipping port for his coal mines in Nanaimo. Today, the heritage buildings and antique shops lend the town a nostalgic feel.

Turning off the highway at Yellow Point Road takes you along the scenic route to Nanaimo, winding through a rural enclave of farms to the sandstone shores of Stuart Channel. Resorts and campgrounds here, at Quennell Lake and on the Nanaimo River offer visitors a variety of experiences.

Top: The Kowutzun Dancers perform on the banks of the Cowichan River at Duncan's Native Heritage Centre.

NANAIMO

Nanaimo's name comes from the Salish word Snenymo for "great and mighty people." Known as the Harbour City, Nanaimo is Vancouver Island's second largest city. Literally and figuratively built on coal, the city sits on rich seams discovered in 1851. The coal brought the first settlers, and in 1852, the Hudson Bay Company erected the bastion to protect them from Native raids. It remains the oldest such structure in North America.

With six deep-sea docks and the BC Ferries terminal at Departure Bay, Nanaimo is the island's largest export centre. Marinas, float plane terminals, commercial fishing boat wharves and Newcastle Island Provincial Marine Park all contribute to the bustle on the sheltered waters of the harbour.

As industry gives way to tourism and a burgeoning population, the city continues to add to its already abundant parkland. The extensive waterfront walkways lead from the fishermen's wharf below the bastion, past the seaplane base and toward Departure Bay. From Georgia Park, the Lion's

Top: Harbour seals play on the rock in the ocean spray.

Bottom left: Nanaimo's famous Bastion was built in 1853 to protect miners from possible native attacks.

Bottom right: A spring lamb frolicks among yellow daffodils.

Top: Viewed from the ferry, the island's lush vegetation is an impressive sight.

Great Bridge crosses the Swy-A-Lana Tidal Lagoon is a favourite warm ocean-water swimming hole. The Queen Elizabeth Promenade continues through Maffeo-Sutton Park with its playgrounds, lawns and benches. Newcastle Island, accessible by ferry from the lagoon from May to October, provides visitors with a tranquil haven from the bustle of town.

Nanaimo's waterfront also appeals to the thousands of sea lions that haul themselves onto the log booms at the Harmac mill in late winter to feed on incoming herring. Wildlife tours from Nanaimo harbour are available. The Morrell Wildlife Sanctuary is a birder's haven, with 11.5 kilometres of trails by beaver ponds and over rocky knolls. The nearby Nanaimo Lakes are another popular recreational choice.

Mute swans swim gracefully through the tranquil waters of Saanich Inlet on a beautiful winter evening.